CENTRAL

D0432036

Fireflies

by Sally M. Walker

CONTRA COSTA COUNTY LIBRARY

Lerner Publications Company • Minneapolis, Minnesota

3 1901 03388 7870

For Marcia Brandt, who asked for a book about fireflies. The answer is: some adult fireflies don't have light organs.

The photographs in this book are reproduced through the courtesy of: © Robert & Linda Mitchell, front cover, pp. 6, 7, 16, 17, 21, 24, 25; © J. E. Lloyd, pp. 4, 12, 14, 15, 19, 20 (inset), 28, 31, 33, 36, 37, 39, 40, 46–47; Visuals Unlimited: (© Bill Beatty) p. 5, (© Jeff J. Daly) pp. 20, 22, (© Bill Banaszewski) p. 42; Photo Researchers, Inc.: (© John Mitchell) p. 8 (left), (© Michael P. Gadomski) pp. 9, 41, (© Dr. Paul A. Zahl) pp. 13, 26, 38, (© Brian Brake) p. 23, (© Kenneth H. Thomas) p. 34, (© Keith Kent/Science Photo Library) p. 43; © Bill Beatty, pp. 8 (right), 30, 34 (inset); © P. Hinchliffe/ Bruce Coleman, Inc., p. 10; © Blythe, R. OSF/Animals Animals, p. 11; © David Liebman, p. 29; © Satoshi Kuribayashi, p. 32.

Thanks to our series consultant, Sharyn Fenwick, elementary science and math specialist. Mrs. Fenwick was the winner of the National Science Teachers Association 1991 Distinguished Teaching Award. She also was the recipient of the Presidential Award for Excellence in Math and Science Teaching, representing the state of Minnesota at the elementary level in 1992.

Text copyright © 2001 by Sally M. Walker

All rights reserved. International copyright secured. No part of this book may be reproduced, stored in a retrieval system, or transmitted in any form or by any means—electronic, mechanical, photocopying, recording, or otherwise—without the prior written permission of Lerner Publications Company, except for the inclusion of brief quotations in an acknowledged review.

Early Bird Nature Books were conceptualized by Ruth Berman and designed by Steve Foley. Series editor is Joelle Riley.

Website address: www.lernerbooks.com

Lerner Publications Company
A division of Lerner Publishing Group
241 First Avenue North
Minneapolis, Minnesota 55401 U.S.A.

Library of Congress Cataloging-in-Publication Data

Walker, Sally M.
    Fireflies / by Sally M. Walker.
      p. cm. — (Early bird nature books)
    Includes index.
    Summary: Describes the physical characteristics, behavior, and life cycle of fireflies.
      ISBN 0-8225-3047-3 (lib. bdg. : alk. paper)
      1. Fireflies—Juvenile literature. [1. Fireflies.] I. Title. II. Series.
QL596.L28 W36 2001
595.76′44-dc21   00-008275

Manufactured in the United States of America
1 2 3 4 5 6 – JR – 06 05 04 03 02 01

Contents

Be a Word Detective

*Can you find these words as you read about the firefly's
life? Be a detective and try to figure out what they mean.
You can turn to the glossary on page 46 for help.*

abdomen	light organs	molt
antennas	luciferase	nocturnal
ATP	luciferin	oxygen
bioluminescence	mandibles	pupa
larvas	maxillas	thorax

*There is more than one way to form plurals of some words.
Words such as* antenna *and* larva *have two possible plural
endings—either an* e *or an* s. *In this book,* s *is used when
many antennas or larvas are being discussed.*

Chapter 1

Some kinds of fireflies sit on trees at night. They blink their lights while they rest there. The trees look like they are on fire. What kind of animal is a firefly?

A Glowing Insect

The moon and stars shine brightly at night. On summer nights, fireflies shine brightly too.

Fireflies are insects. Insects have three main body parts. They have a head, a thorax, and an abdomen (AB-duh-muhn). Insects also have six legs. Most insects have one or two pairs of wings. An insect's skeleton is on the outside of its body. It is not on the inside like a person's skeleton.

Fireflies are sometimes called lightning bugs.

Fireflies are not flies. They are beetles. Beetles are insects with two pairs of wings. The front pair is stiff. It protects the back pair of wings. Other beetles are ladybugs, potato beetles, and dung beetles. Fireflies' skeletons are softer than those of most other beetles.

Fireflies are beetles. A Colorado potato beetle (above) is resting on a leaf. A ladybug (right) is another type of beetle.

Fireflies live in fields like this one. During the day, fireflies stay hidden in the grass.

Scientists have found over 2,000 species, or kinds, of fireflies. Fireflies live in almost every part of the world. But they do not live in places where it is very dry or very cold all year. Fireflies live in the grass and around bushes. They also live along the edges of forests.

Most fireflies can glow when they are adults.

Fireflies are different from most insects in a special way. Fireflies glow. A firefly's light glows yellow or yellowish green.

All fireflies glow when they are young. Most species of fireflies can glow when they are adults, too.

An adult firefly can make its light blink on and off. Each species of firefly has its own pattern of flashes. Males and females of each species use the flashes to find each other.

A glowing female firefly waits in the grass.

Most fireflies are nocturnal. Nocturnal creatures are active at night. During the day, most fireflies stay under leaves or rocks, or in the grass. Soon after sunset, males fly away from their hiding places. They zigzag through the air.

The fireflies shown here have just left their hiding places.

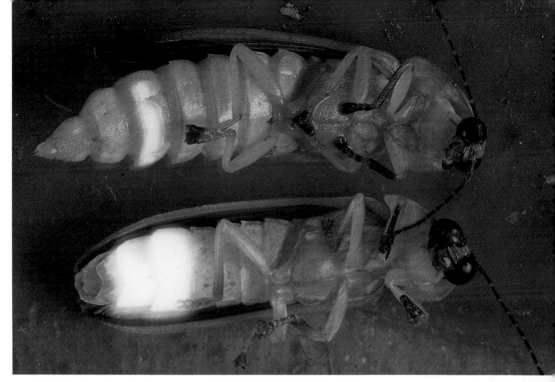

A female firefly (top) *is usually bigger than a male* (bottom).

Female fireflies usually wait near the ground. They climb on grass and on other plants. A female watches the pattern of a male's blinking light. If he is the same species as she is, she blinks once at him.

Fireflies don't blink all night long. The males and females of some species flash at each other for about 20 minutes. Other species may blink for several hours.

Chapter 2

This firefly's scientific name is Photuris lucicrescens. *How many antennas does a firefly have?*

Body Parts

A firefly has two large eyes on its head. Each eye has many flat places on it. Imagine looking at yourself in a cracked mirror. The cracks make it look as though you are made of many bits and pieces. That's how scientists think fireflies see things.

A firefly has two antennas (an-TEH-nuhz) on its head. Fireflies use the antennas to touch and smell things. The antennas help fireflies find out what is around them.

Long, thick antennas help fireflies to sense objects.

Fireflies have a shield that covers their head.

A firefly's head has two sharp jaws that grab objects. The jaws are called mandibles (MAN-duh-buhlz). Fireflies use their mandibles to catch food.

Fireflies have no teeth. Instead, they have maxillas (mak-SIH-luhz). Fireflies chew with their maxillas. The maxillas are behind the mandibles.

16

Behind a firefly's head is its thorax. A firefly's legs are attached to its thorax. Fireflies have six legs. Each leg has a foot with two claws. Fireflies use their claws to climb trees and grass.

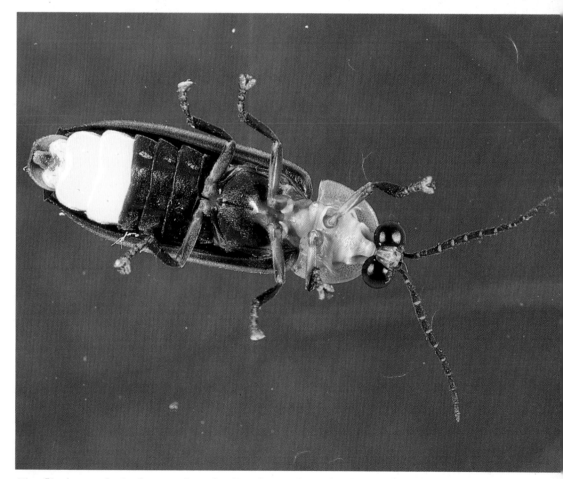

Fireflies use their feet to brush dirt from their body.

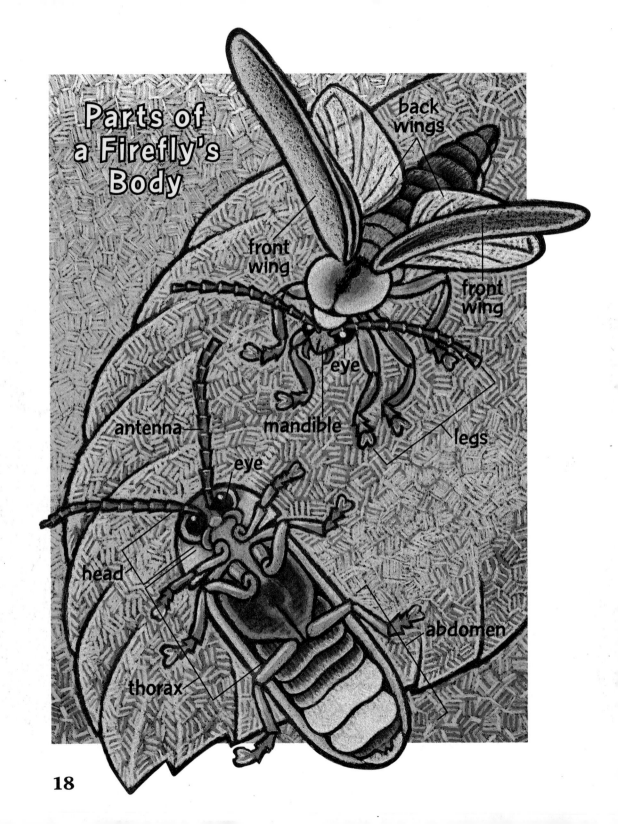

Parts of a Firefly's Body

back wings

front wing

front wing

eye

antenna

mandible

legs

eye

head

abdomen

thorax

18

A firefly has two pairs of wings. They are attached to the thorax. A firefly has front wings and back wings. When a firefly is resting, the front wings cover and protect the back wings. A firefly uses its back wings for flying.

A firefly is getting ready to fly from a leaf.

A firefly's front wings are harder than its back wings.
Inset: *The females of some species of fireflies have no wings.*

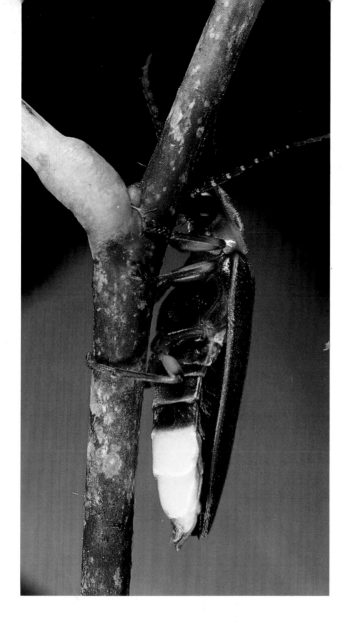

Fireflies breathe through tiny holes on the sides of their abdomen.

Behind a firefly's thorax is its abdomen. A firefly's light organs are on the bottom of its abdomen. The light organs are the parts of a firefly that glow.

Chapter 3

Fireflies can light up a room. What is the light made by living things called?

Making Light

A firefly's light is called bioluminescence (bye-oh-loo-muh-NEH-suhnts). Bioluminescence is light made by living things. Bioluminescence is different from the lights we have in our homes.

We use electric lamps in our homes. Electric lamps give off two kinds of energy. Light is one kind of energy. Heat is the other kind of energy. A lightbulb gives off bright light. But most of the energy that comes from a lightbulb is heat.

Glowing insects light up this cave in the country of New Zealand.

It is easy to see a firefly's light organs when they are lit up. Some female fireflies have no light organs.

Bioluminescence is cold light. Fireflies do not use electricity to make light. A firefly makes light by mixing chemicals (KEM-uh-kuhlz) inside its body. When the chemicals mix, they make energy. Almost all of the energy the chemicals make is light energy. Only a tiny bit is heat energy. That's why fireflies are cool when you touch them.

Fireflies use four chemicals to make light. First, a firefly needs oxygen (AHK-sih-juhn). Oxygen is a gas in the air. Most creatures need oxygen to live. We use our lungs to get oxygen from the air. A firefly has small holes on its abdomen that let in oxygen.

Different species of fireflies have different numbers of light organs.

Second, a firefly needs ATP. ATP is a chemical found in all living things. ATP controls how bright a firefly's light is. If a firefly has a lot of ATP, its light is brighter and more yellow.

The other two chemicals a firefly needs to make light are luciferin (loo-SIH-fuh-rihn) and luciferase (loo-SIH-fuh-rays). A firefly makes luciferin and luciferase in its abdomen.

Luciferase makes other chemicals work together to make light.

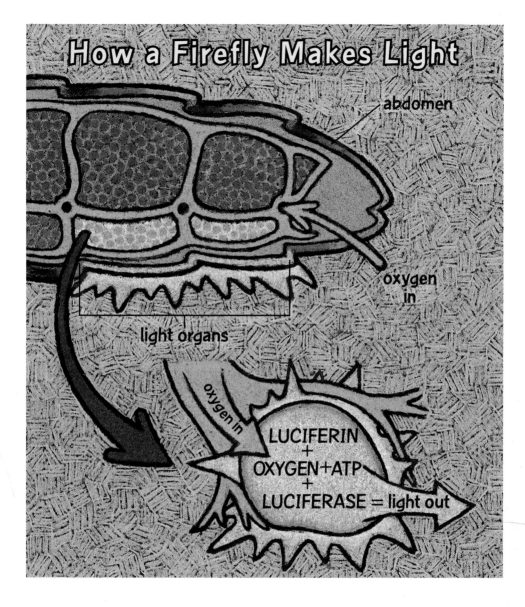

How a Firefly Makes Light

abdomen

oxygen in

light organs

oxygen in

LUCIFERIN
+
OXYGEN+ATP
+
LUCIFERASE = light out

Oxygen, ATP, luciferin, and luciferase mix in a firefly's light organs. When these chemicals mix, they make a tiny flash of light.

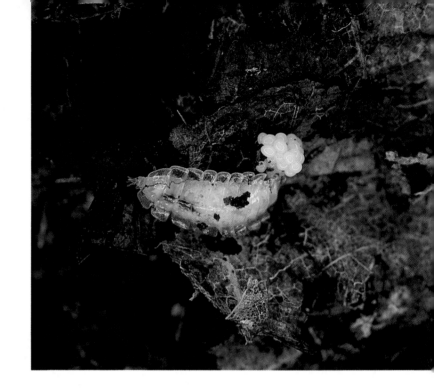

Chapter 4

Different species of fireflies lay different numbers of eggs. Female fireflies lay from 40 to 1,000 eggs at a time. When does a firefly lay her eggs?

Growing Up

Baby fireflies hatch from eggs. A female firefly lays eggs in the summer. She lays her eggs in loose, damp soil. The soil keeps the eggs safe from the sun's heat and light.

Each egg is round, soft, and smooth. Eggs from some species glow dimly. The glowing eggs do not blink. In about 28 days, the eggs hatch.

Newly hatched fireflies are called larvas (LAR-vuhz). Larvas do not look like adult fireflies. They look like ridgy worms.

Larvas hide and sleep during the day. They hunt for food at night. A larva eats a lot. It eats snails, earthworms, slugs, and soft insects.

This is a firefly larva. The larvas of some species of fireflies live on land. Others live in the water.

A hungry larva is chewing on a slug.

A larva pinches its prey with its mandibles. The larva squirts a liquid through its mandibles and into the animal. The liquid turns the animal's muscles into a goopy, thick liquid. The larva sucks out the mushy liquid.

The meal helps the larva grow. Its growing body becomes too big for its skin. Then the larva molts. When it molts, it sheds its old, tight skin. The old skin splits. The larva wriggles out of the old skin. New skin already covers the larva.

The larva grows all summer. It molts several times as it grows. It sleeps during the next winter. Then the larva wakes up in the spring. The larvas of some species are ready to begin changing into adults. But other species will spend another summer and winter as larvas.

A larva grabbed this snail with its strong mandibles. The larva has eaten its way deep inside the snail's shell.

A firefly's shelter may be on top of the ground. Or it may be just below the ground.

In the spring, the larva builds a shelter. A shelter is a safe place that is covered. The larva makes its shelter out of mud. The larva chews a mouthful of soil until it becomes wet mud. The larva spits the mud out in strips. It does this many times. The larva piles strips on top of each other to make its shelter. When the shelter is finished, it looks like a bowl turned upside down.

A larva molts for the last time. It is changing into a pupa. This firefly is not inside a shelter. But most fireflies molt inside their shelter.

The larva crawls inside the shelter and curls up. The larva stays still for about 40 days. Then it molts one last time. A stiff white cover forms around its body. The larva has changed into a pupa (PYOO-puh).

The pupas shown here are becoming adult fireflies.

The pupa lies on its back inside the shelter. Important changes are taking place. The pupa is growing adult antennas, eyes, legs, and light organs. It is also growing wings. In 10 days, the pupa's cover splits open. The pupa has become an adult firefly.

The Life
of a
Firefly

adult

eggs

pupa

larva

It will take a few hours for this tan-colored firefly to darken.

The new adult firefly is white or tan. In a few hours, it turns brown or gray. The firefly stays in its shelter for a few days. Its legs and wings get stronger. When the firefly is ready, it chews its way out of the shelter.

Adult fireflies live only about 5 to 30 days. Most adult fireflies do not eat or drink. A few species of fireflies eat the sweet liquid found in flowers. Some drink water. Females of some species eat other fireflies.

This firefly is ready to begin life as an adult.

Chapter 5

A lizard gobbles up a firefly. Lizards eat adult and baby fireflies. What other animal enemies do fireflies have?

Dangers to Fireflies

Fireflies have many animal enemies. Toads, insects, spiders, lizards, and some birds eat fireflies. Fish and frogs eat fireflies who fall into the water.

Sometimes fireflies can fly away from danger. Or they can hide.

This firefly landed in a spider's sticky web. The spider is attacking the firefly.

Male fireflies of some species protect themselves in a special way. They make a liquid inside their bodies. The liquid is poisonous. It tastes bad to birds, lizards, frogs, and spiders. When one of these animals tries to eat a firefly, it spits it back out. If it doesn't spit out the firefly, it will become very sick. The animal learns to avoid eating fireflies.

A female firefly eats a male firefly. Females who eat
males are in the Photuris *group of fireflies.*

Female fireflies cannot make this bad-
tasting liquid. But the females of some species
get the liquid in a tricky way. They eat male
fireflies who make the liquid. Then the females
taste bad, too.

Scientists think a firefly's light may help to protect it. If an animal enemy sees the firefly's glow, it may leave it alone.

Most firefly eggs, larvas, pupas, and adults glow. Animals like this American toad may leave a glowing firefly alone.

People are cutting down a forest where fireflies live to build a pond.

People can be a danger to fireflies. People use sprays to kill harmful insects. These sprays often kill fireflies, too. People also hurt fireflies when they build cities. It is hard for fireflies to live in a city.

Fireflies fly slowly through the night air.

Fireflies may live near your home. Watch the fireflies as they fly. Count their flashes. Follow them as they crawl in the grass and on bushes. You will discover that fireflies are amazing insects.

On Sharing a Book

As you know, adults greatly influence a child's attitude toward reading. When a child sees you read, or when you share a book with a child, you're sending a message that reading is important. Show the child that reading a book together is important to you. Find a comfortable, quiet place. Turn off the television and limit other distractions, such as telephone calls.

Be prepared to start slowly. Take turns reading parts of this book. Stop and talk about what you're reading. Talk about the photographs. You may find that much of the shared time is spent discussing just a few pages. This discussion time is valuable for both of you, so don't move through the book too quickly. If the child begins to lose interest, stop reading. Continue sharing the book at another time. When you do pick up the book again, be sure to revisit the parts you have already read. Most importantly, enjoy the book!

Be a Vocabulary Detective

You will find a word list on page 5. Words selected for this list are important to the understanding of the topic of this book. Encourage the child to be a word detective and search for the words as you read the book together. Talk about what the words mean and how they are used in the sentence. Do any of these words have more than one meaning? You will find these words defined in a glossary on page 46.

What about Questions?

Use questions to make sure the child understands the information in this book. Here are some suggestions:

What did this paragraph tell us? What does this picture show? What do you think we'll learn about next? What kind of animal is a firefly? Which animals are related to fireflies? Could fireflies live near your home? What do objects look like to fireflies? How many pairs of wings do fireflies have? Why do fireflies blink their lights? Where are a firefly's light organs? How do fireflies make light? How is a firefly larva different from an adult firefly? How does a larva build its shelter? What animal enemies do fireflies have? What is your favorite part of the book? Why?

If the child has questions, don't hesitate to respond with questions of your own such as: What do *you* think? Why? What is it that you don't know? If the child can't remember certain facts, turn to the index.

Introducing the Index

The index is an important learning tool. It helps readers get information quickly without searching throughout the whole book. Turn to the index on page 47. Choose an entry, such as *enemies,* and ask the child to use the index to find out what enemies a firefly has. Repeat this exercise with as many entries as you like. Ask the child to point out the differences between an index and a glossary. (The index helps readers find information quickly, while the glossary tells readers what words mean.)

All the World in Metric!

Although our monetary system is in metric units (based on multiples of 10), the United States is one of the few countries in the world that does not use the metric system of measurement. Here are some conversion activities you and the child can do using a calculator:

WHEN YOU KNOW:	MULTIPLY BY:	TO FIND:
miles	1.609	kilometers
feet	0.3048	meters
inches	2.54	centimeters
gallons	3.787	liters
tons	0.907	metric tons
pounds	0.454	kilograms

Activities

Make up a story about a firefly. Be sure to include information from this book. Draw or paint pictures to illustrate your story.

Watch fireflies blinking their lights outside. Can you see female fireflies answering males? Take a flashlight and try to imitate the pattern of one of the fireflies you see.

Gently catch some fireflies and put them in a jar. Touch a firefly. Is is warm or cold? Turn off the lights. Are the fireflies glowing? Can you see yourself in the mirror with just the light from the fireflies?

Glossary

abdomen (AB-duh-muhn)—the back part of a firefly's body

antennas (an-TEH-nuhz)—the feelers on a firefly's head

ATP—a chemical that provides energy for all living things

bioluminescence (bye-oh-loo-muh-NEH-suhnts)—light made by living things

larvas (LAR-vuhz)—fireflies in their second stage of growth

light organs—the parts of a firefly that glow

luciferase (loo-SIH-fuh-rays)—a chemical that fireflies use to make light

luciferin (loo-SIH-fuh-rihn)—a chemical that fireflies use to make light

mandibles (MAN-duh-buhlz)—a firefly's sharp jaws

maxillas (mak-SIH-luhz)—parts that fireflies use to chew food

molt—to shed old skin

nocturnal—active at night

oxygen (AHK-sih-juhn)—a gas most creatures need to live

pupa (PYOO-puh)—a firefly in its third stage of growth

thorax—the middle part of a firefly's body

Index

Pages listed in **bold** type refer to photographs.

About the Author

Sally M. Walker is the author of many books for young readers, including the early readers *Mary Anning: Fossil Hunter* and *The 18 Penny Goose*. When she isn't busy writing and doing research for books, Ms. Walker works as a children's literature consultant. She has taught children's literature at Northern Illinois University and has given presentations at many reading conferences. While she writes, Ms. Walker shares desk space with her family's two cats, who sit next to the computer and look out the window at birds in the backyard. She lives in Illinois with her husband and two children.

The Early Bird Nature Books Series

African Elephants
Alligators
Ants
Apple Trees
Bobcats
Brown Bears
Cats
Cockroaches
Cougars
Crayfish
Dandelions
Dolphins
Fireflies
Giant Pandas
Giant Sequoia Trees

Herons
Horses
Jellyfish
Manatees
Moose
Mountain Goats
Mountain Gorillas
Ostriches
Peacocks
Penguins
Polar Bears
Popcorn Plants
Prairie Dogs
Rats
Red-Eyed Tree Frogs

Saguaro Cactus
Sandhill Cranes
Scorpions
Sea Lions
Sea Turtles
Slugs
Swans
Tarantulas
Tigers
Venus Flytraps
Vultures
Walruses
Whales
Wild Turkeys
Zebras